DESTINATION
NEW ORLEANS

by Martin Hintz

Lerner Publications Company • Minneapolis

PHOTO ACKNOWLEDGMENTS
Cover photo by Alex Demyan. All inside photos courtesy of © Robert Holmes, pp. 5, 12, 65, 72 (both); Buddy Mays/TRAVEL STOCK, pp. 6, 11; © CC Lockwood/DDB Photo Stock, pp. 8-9; Minneapolis Public Library and Information Center, p. 10; © Port of New Orleans/Donn Young–Port Photographer, pp. 16 (bottom), 19 (both), 20 (top), 46, 56, 57 (all); © Betty Crowell, pp. 16 (top), 18-19, 21, 55, 56 (bottom); © Michele Burgess, pp. 20 (bottom), 23, 27; © David Sailors, pp. 24-25; Alex Demyan, pp. 26, 50, 63, 64, 70-71; © William B. Folsom, p. 28; The Historic New Orleans Collection, pp. 31, 33, 35, 38, 40, 41, 42, 44, 44-45, 47, 49; Archive Photos, p. 32; Corbis-Bettmann, p. 43; UPI/Corbis-Bettmann, p. 48; Avondale Shipyards, p. 53; Silocaf of New Orleans, Inc., p. 53; Archive Photos/Reuters, p. 58; Louisiana Office of Tourism, pp. 66, 69; Reuters/Corbis-Bettmann, p. 73; © David G. Houser, p. 74. Maps by Ortelius Design.

For those early folks who preferred Louisiana to the Bastille.

Copyright © 1997 by Lerner Publications Company

All rights reserved. International copyright secured. No part of this book may be reproduced, stored in a retrieval system, or transmitted in any form or by any means—electronic, mechanical, photocopying, recording, or otherwise— without the prior written permission of Lerner Publications Company, except for the inclusion of brief quotations in an acknowledged review.

LIBRARY OF CONGRESS CATALOGING-IN-PUBLICATION DATA

Hintz, Martin.
   Destination New Orleans / by Martin Hintz.
      p.   cm. — (Port cities of North America)
   Includes index.
   Summary: Discusses the geology, history, economy, and daily life of New Orleans.
   ISBN 0-8225-2784-7 (lib. bdg. : alk. paper)
   New Orleans (La.) — Juvenile literature. [1. New Orleans (La.)] I. Title. II. Series.
F379.N557D47   1997
976.3'35—dc20   96-16306

Manufactured in the United States of America
1 2 3 4 5 6 – JR – 02 01 00 99 98 97

The glossary that begins on page 76 gives definitions of words shown in **bold type** in the text.

CONTENTS

CHAPTER ONE	Lay of the Land	7
CHAPTER TWO	Historic New Orleans	29
CHAPTER THREE	The Port at Work	51
CHAPTER FOUR	The Big Easy	67
	Glossary	76
	Pronunciation Guide	77
	Index	78
	About the Author	80

CHAPTER ONE

LAY OF THE LAND

Situated in Louisiana on the mighty Mississippi River, New Orleans was born because its European founders wanted to make money—oodles of it. The early settlers favored building a great city near where the river empties into the Gulf of Mexico. The river and the Gulf formed a watery highway to the wide Atlantic Ocean. Ships could carry goods from the interior of North America to ports around the world.

The Native Americans living in the area when the first European explorers arrived in the 1500s already knew that southern Louisiana was a prime spot for commerce. Nature's bounty included furs, fish, and oyster shells. For hundreds of years, the Indians' long, sleek canoes easily slid through the region's inlets

Riverboats (facing page) *are a familiar sight on the Mississippi River. They line the shores near downtown New Orleans.*

and **bayous** (water passages without currents). These early merchants traveled up the Mississippi to trade these goods with other Native American nations farther upriver.

But larger European vessels had a harder time navigating the challenging Mississippi. Sandbars often blocked the mouth of the river where it spills into the Gulf. So a site for a port city was eventually selected on higher ground, 110 miles north of the Gulf, far from the natural obstacle.

Here New Orleans—also known as the Crescent City—grew on a marshy piece of land shaped like a semicircle and tucked between the Mississippi River and shallow Lake Pontchartrain. Bridges and several narrow land passages join the city to the rest of Louisiana.

Louisiana, in turn, is situated in the Deep South. The state's neighbors include Texas to the west, Arkansas to the north, and Mississippi to the east. The Gulf of Mexico lies directly south of Louisiana. But in the city of New Orleans, all eyes are on the river.

Father of Waters

What is so important about the Mississippi? One of North America's great rivers, the Mississippi stretches for 2,340 long, muddy miles through the Central Plains of the United States, from Minnesota to Louisiana. The river ranks as one of the most extensive water systems in the world, linking communities all across North America to the Atlantic Ocean by way of the Gulf.

Remarkably, the mighty Mississippi starts as a tiny stream trickling from Lake Itasca, a small lake in part of northwestern Minnesota.

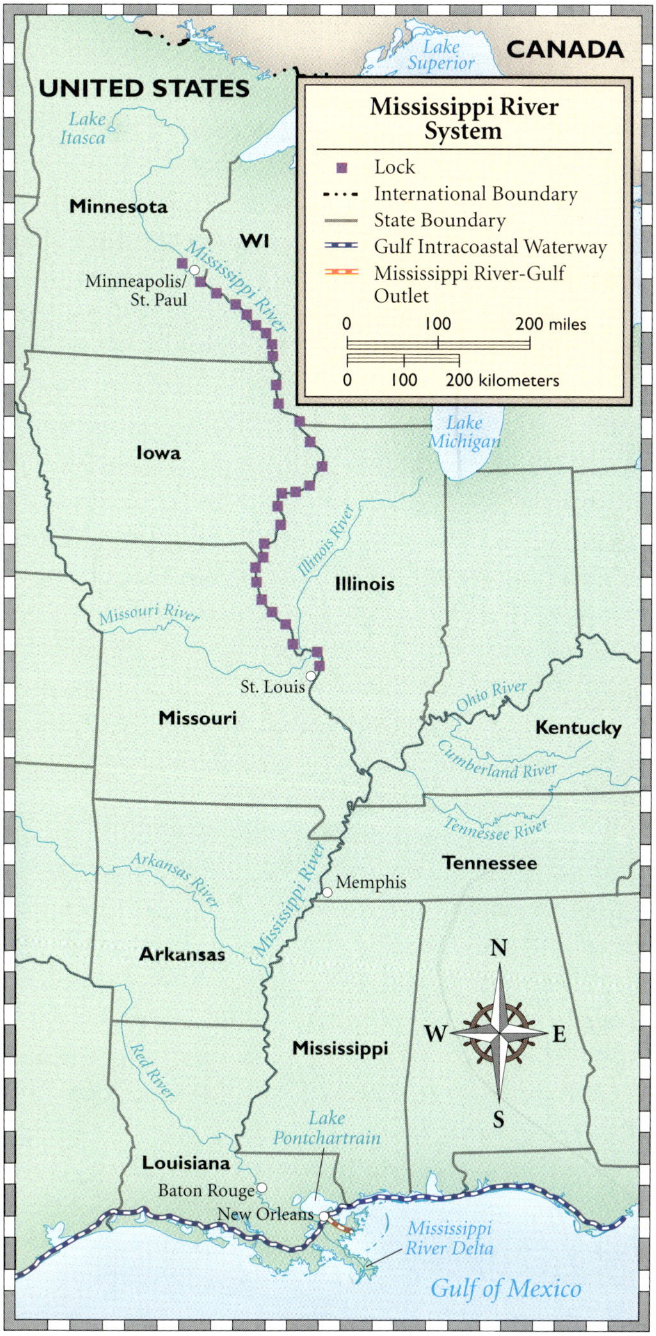

Meandering bayous (above) *are characteristic of the lower Mississippi River and its* **delta** *where the river fans out to meet the Gulf of Mexico. This map* (right) *shows the full course of the river and its tributaries from its start in Minnesota to where it empties just south of New Orleans. The Mississippi winds for 2,340 miles through the most productive agricultural and industrial areas of the central United States.*

The river is named for the Algonquin Indian words *misi sipi,* meaning "great water." The river is also sometimes referred to as the Father of Waters. This is for good reason. The Mississippi's **basin** (area drained by a river system) encompasses a total of nearly 1.25 million square miles—the entire midsection of the United States. On its way south, the river takes in millions of gallons of water from 300 smaller rivers or streams. These smaller rivers, called tributaries, pour into the Mississippi from 31 states. As the churning river rolls along, it grows deeper, wilder, and stronger.

Some of the Mississippi's major tributaries are the Illinois, Missouri, Ohio, Cumberland, Tennessee, Arkansas, and Red Rivers. These rivers, along with the **Gulf Intracoastal Waterway** (an artificial water system stretching from Texas to Florida), form a vast network of navigable inland waterways that links New Orleans to the rest of the United States. The total length of the network measures 14,500 miles.

In addition to the water the Mississippi collects as it flows toward the Gulf, the river picks up millions of tons of dirt and mud. At the mouth of the river, where it seeps into the Gulf, the sediments add to a huge delta, or wide, muddy plain. Geologists say enough silt is deposited at the mouth of the Mississippi each year to spread an inch-thick layer across 5,000 square miles of land.

New Orleans's neighborhoods were built wherever ground could be found. The oldest section of the city—known as the French Quarter, or the Vieux Carré—sits about 12 feet above sea level, while most other parts of town are

In northern Minnesota, the Mississippi River begins its long journey, starting out as a small stream flowing out of Lake Itasca.

▶ Lake Pontchartrain has affected the growth of New Orleans. The lake—40 miles long, 24 miles wide, and 16 feet deep—is the seventh largest in the United States. The lake's position means that the city can't expand northward. With the river bending around the other three sides of the crescent, New Orleans can't grow outward as many inland communities do.

▶ The Mississippi River is 2,200 feet wide and 150 feet deep near the foot of Canal Street, one of the city's major roadways. Slightly downriver, near Algiers Point, the river is more than 200 feet deep.

The oldest neighborhood of New Orleans is the French Quarter. In the late 1700s, when New Orleans was under Spanish rule, the original French Quarter burned down twice. The neighborhood's Spanish architecture dates from this period.

below sea level. What's more, the marshy land beneath New Orleans continues to settle slowly, causing the city to sink an average of three inches each century. Jokesters kid that in a thousand years the colorful Mardi Gras celebration will be a parade of motorboats! Kidding aside, flooding is a danger in some parts of New Orleans.

The bedrock (natural rocky land surface) sits 70 feet below the water, sand, silt, and mud in which New Orleans wriggles its toes. North of Lake Pontchartrain, however, an outcropping of bedrock supports the suburbs of Covington, Madisonville, and Mandeville. People there don't have to worry about flooding because

they are above sea level. From this side of the lake, the rock gradually disappears under the water. No bedrock can be seen in New Orleans at all.

Safeguarding the City

Many portions of New Orleans exist because of well-developed construction and engineering systems. Protecting the city and the port facilities of New Orleans are **levees.** These earthen dikes, topped with concrete, ring the city. The U.S. Army Corps of Engineers has built levees to help control river flooding and to protect the lakefront from hurricanes.

Another annual danger is the arrival of the northern snowmelt, which adds to the river's volume in a great surge of water. To safeguard the below-sea-level city from the river's surge, the tops of the riverfront levees are 20 feet above sea level. Along the **Industrial Canal,** an artificial outlet between the Mississippi and Lake Pontchartrain, the levee height varies from 12.5 to 14 feet. At Lake Pontchartrain, the levees range from 17.5 to 20 feet above sea level. Massive gates exist in these floodwalls, which can be closed to prevent high waters from flooding the low-lying land inside the levee. Usually open, the gates allow access to parking lots, railroad tracks, and wharves.

But New Orleans still faces other natural dangers. Hurricanes kick up waves that roll over the top of the seawall lining the lakeshore. When these powerful windstorms and rainstorms roar in from the Gulf, residents south of New Orleans evacuate to higher land to the north.

Consider this scenario: An extreme hurricane forms in the western Gulf of Mexico and heads

Much of New Orleans lies below sea level and is subject to flooding. Concrete levees that surround the city protect neighborhoods from the floodwaters of several nearby lakes and rivers.

slowly northeastward to the narrow passageway between Lake Pontchartrain and the Gulf. Then the hurricane stalls. If this scenario occurred, lake waters could top the levees and flood the city. Because New Orleans is nearly surrounded by water, the greatest difficulty in the event of a monster hurricane would be evacuating people across the few bridges leading out of town.

A Sprawling Port ▶ The Port of New Orleans stretches from Nashville to France—well, sort of. Just look at a map of the city. Port facilities sprawl across 22 miles of waterfront. The facilities go from the Nashville Avenue Wharf in uptown New Orleans to the France Road container complex on the Industrial Canal in eastern New Orleans. The Industrial Canal also connects with the eastward channel of the Gulf Intracoastal Waterway and with the **Mississippi River–Gulf Outlet.** Ships prefer to use the MRGO, as locals call the channel, because its route to the Gulf is 40 miles shorter than traveling via the river.

Lining the water in these areas are a string of wharves, or structures where ships dock to load and unload cargo and passengers. Each wharf has its own unique combination of facilities—such as transportation links or loading equipment—which make for easy handling of forest products, food, steel, coffee, textiles, resins, rubber, and other commodities. Most wharves handle general cargo, but others—called **dedicated wharves**—specialize. Heavy duty steel, for example, must use wharves that are strong enough to withstand the weighty cargo.

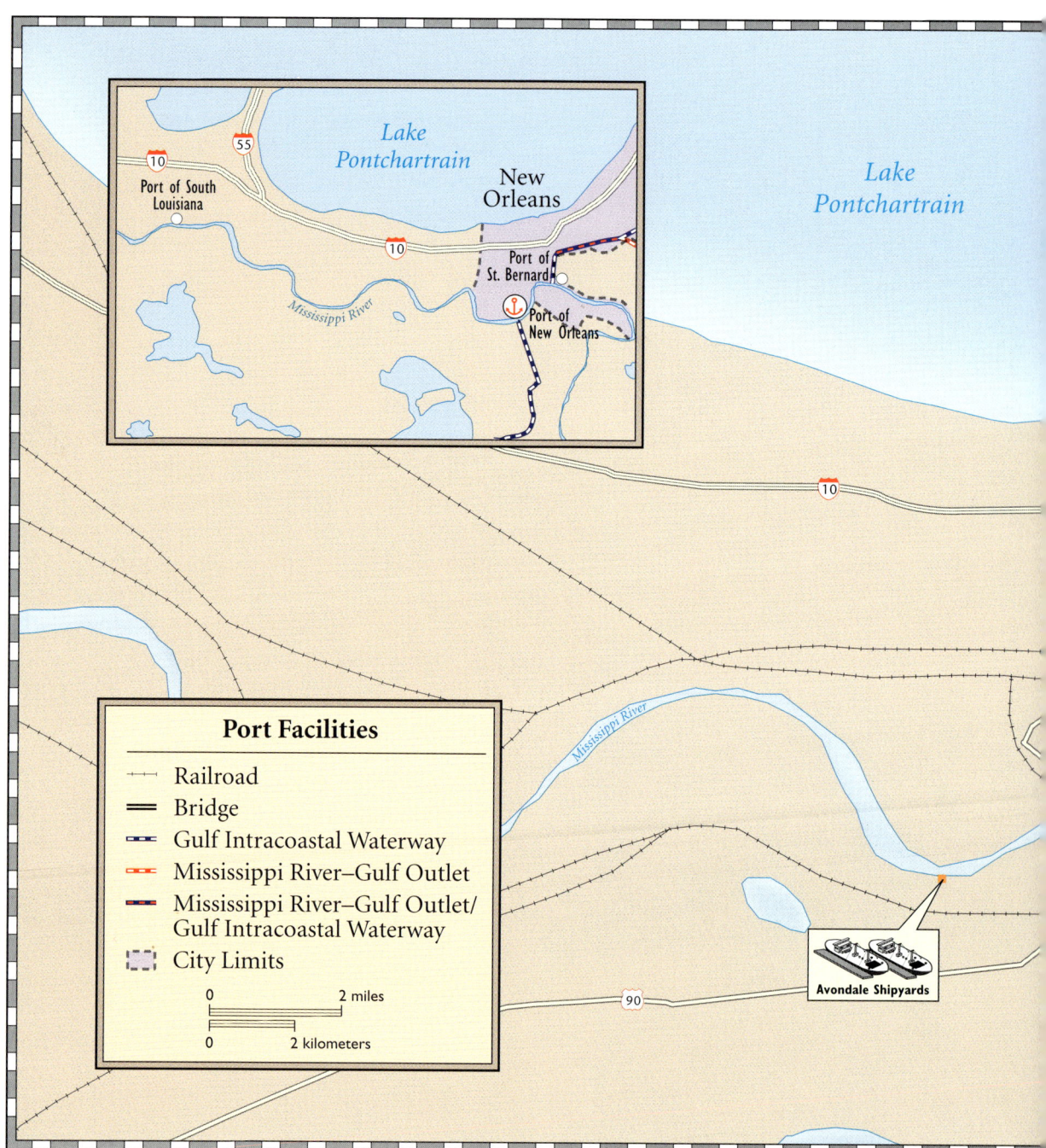

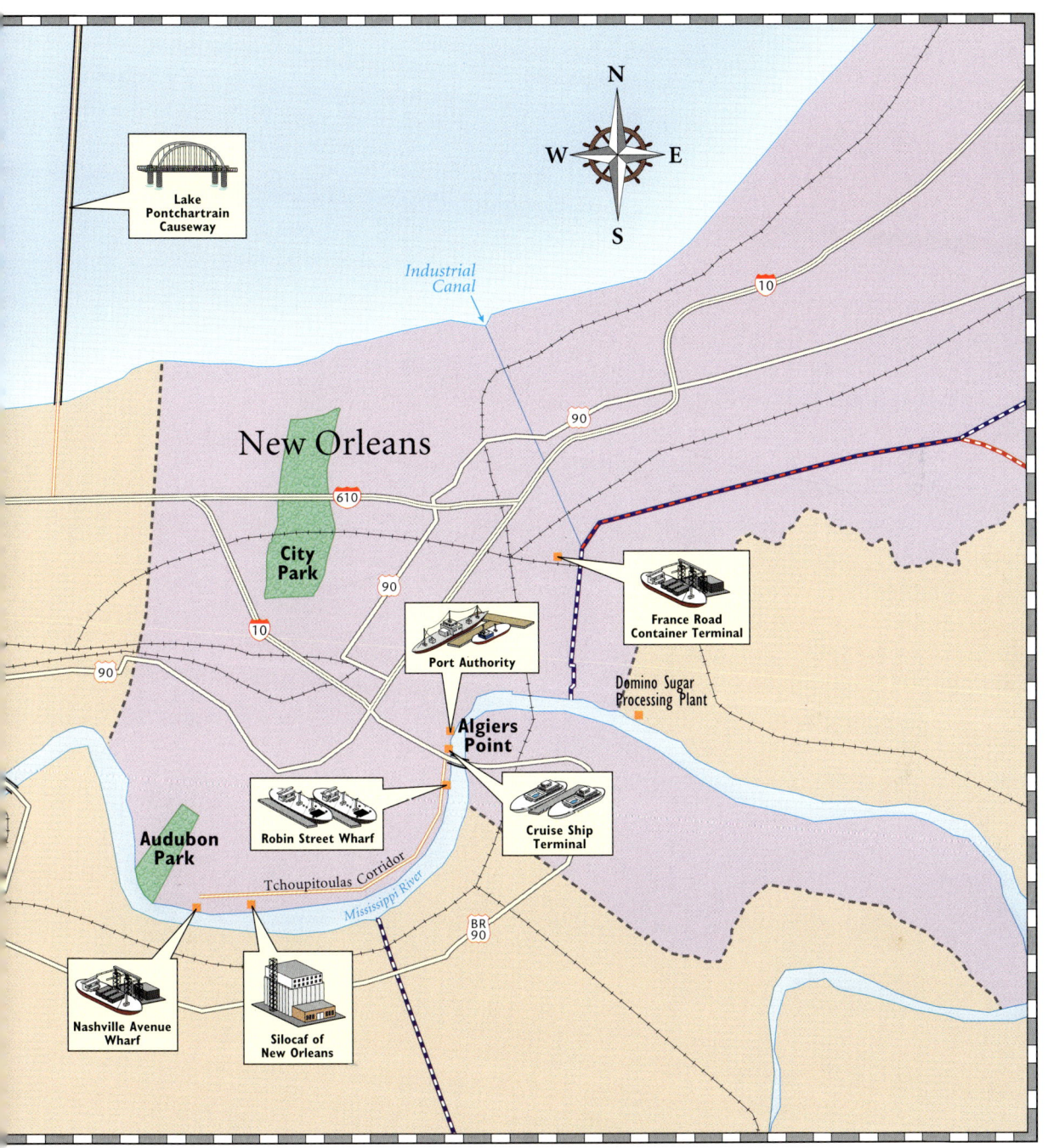

Another example of a dedicated wharf is the Cruise Ship Terminal. It handles the many cruise liners that pause in New Orleans so that passengers can sightsee.

Like other modern ports, New Orleans receives many cargoes packed in heavy metal boxes called containers. Giant cranes pick up the boxes from a ship's deep cargo hold, or storage space. The cranes carefully lower the containers onto truck trailers. On some docks, trains can pull up alongside the ships. Cranes then load the flatcars with containers.

Other cargo is also quickly loaded and unloaded at New Orleans's modern public and private port facilities. Fuel oil, gas, and other bulk liquid products travel ship to shore, or vice versa, by means of large hoses. The liquid is then stored in huge round tanks. To load grain, ships pull up near storage units called grain elevators. Conveyor belts or chutes transfer corn, soybeans, or wheat into a ship's hold. Millions of bushels of grain can be loaded in a few hours this way.

Container cargo (below) *is ready to be unloaded. The* ***Industrial Canal*** *(bottom) links the Mississippi River–Gulf Outlet (MRGO) and the Gulf Intracoastal Waterway, which provides an inland water route from Texas to Florida.*

CONTEMPORARY CANAL

For years New Orleans lacked an efficient connection between the Mississippi River and Lake Pontchartrain. In the 1920s, workers dug the Industrial Canal to link the two bodies of water. A lock system within the canal raised and lowered ships to the next level of the waterway.

This system worked well for awhile, but in 1944 the Industrial Canal became an important link in the Gulf Intracoastal Waterway, which provides a path from Texas to Florida for barges. Barge traffic increased, and barges were built bigger. Traffic jams became common. Nevertheless, shippers still wanted to use New Orleans's waterways. But the existing locks needed to be widened and modernized.

Coming up with a solution wasn't easy. The U.S. Congress passed the Federal River and Harbor Act of 1956, which authorized the U.S. Army Corps of Engineers to replace the Industrial Canal lock. But the first plan would have destroyed 10,000 acres of wetlands, which are home to hundreds of species of birds and animals. A 1982 plan, which would have uprooted residents of New Orleans's historic Holy Cross and Lower Ninth Ward neighborhoods, was also dismissed.

In the early 1990s, yet another plan was in its last stages of approval. Under this proposal, barge traffic would continue through the existing locks during construction, keeping the commercial sector happy. No homes would be demolished, and construction noise would be reduced because workers would put up prefabricated structures rather than build them on site. If approved, the construction will take 10 years to complete and will cost $450 million. The plan will triple the amount of cargo able to go through the new facilities, guaranteeing that New Orleans will continue as a busy, flourishing port.

Efficient and reliable dockside cargo handling allows for faster delivery, cutting the need for warehouse storage. Shipping company owners and port officials are always seeking faster and more cost-efficient means for moving products. Some oceangoing ships, called LASH (Lighter Aboard Ship) vessels, carry fully loaded river barges that are lifted aboard by powerful straddle cranes. When these vessels reach their destination, the barges are simply removed from the mother ship and hauled away by tugs.

Altogether the Port of New Orleans regulates 88 miles of waterfront, and the port itself offers 50 berths, or anchoring spots, at wharves. (Other wharves are privately owned but under the port's jurisdiction.) Each year more than 2,500 vessels representing 70 international steamship companies call at New Orleans to load and unload cargo at these berths.

Getting Products to Markets

These large, oceangoing ships cannot reach the inland regions of the United States because of their hull's depth requirements. Northward from the state capital of Baton Rouge, where the river is more shallow, barges, tugboats, and towboats take over. Barges are sturdy, flat-bottomed boats that are an especially important means of hauling goods along the inland waterway system of the United States. Tugs and towboats assist barges by pushing or pulling anywhere from 1 to 50 of the heavy boats along the Mississippi. The towboat and its barges together are called a tow. Sixteen companies move barges through the Port of New Orleans. More than 100,000 barges visit the port each year.

LASH vessels (below) *ferry small barges across the ocean. Then cranes remove the barges, which tugboats push upstream. Many train* (above) *and truck lines service the port. Steel* (right) *is one of the chief commodities shipped through New Orleans.*

Grain, coal, and chemicals are shipped to the Port of New Orleans from the northern United States. Crude petroleum, steel products, and rubber make the return trip to the industrial heartland. A single barge can carry 1,500 tons of this cargo—as much as what 15 railcars or 60 semitrailer trucks can handle!

Covered hopper barges move products such as food, sand, and paper that must be protected from the weather. Open barges hold coal. Tank barges carry molasses, petroleum, and other fluids. Deck barges haul heavy machinery and other bulk items. Some deck barges are small enough to be hoisted fully loaded aboard oceangoing freighters. These barges can be unloaded in an overseas port and then used to distribute goods by river in another country.

But not all markets are connected by water, and barges move more slowly than trains or trucks do. So railways and roadways are also important components of port trade. Six major railroad companies serve the New Orleans port. CSX Transportation links the facility to 20 states, the District of Columbia, and the Canadian province of Ontario. CSX has 18,800 miles

of rails. Other railroads serving the Port of New Orleans are Kansas City Southern, Illinois Central, Norfolk Southern, Southern Pacific, and Union Pacific.

About 75 truck lines also serve the port, picking up dry, refrigerated, and liquid cargoes for short trips to nearby cities or for long cross-country hauls. The Tchoupitoulas Corridor, a road built in the mid-1990s on both sides of the riverfront levees, steers port and other traffic away from city streets. This corridor gives truckers quick access to the freeways. To cut congestion, the two lanes on the city's side of the corridor are reserved for local traffic and the two lanes on the river's side are designated for port traffic.

Governing and managing the port is the responsibility of a seven-member board of commissioners, with 420 office and field personnel. The board sets policies, while the staff manages the daily operations of the port.

◀ **Who's in Charge?**

The Tchoupitoulas Corridor (facing page, top) *allows trucks to move between the port and nearby highways. A tug and barge* (right) *await the opening of the lock so they can proceed downriver.*

Other governmental agencies also help keep the Port of New Orleans safe and running smoothly. With 1,200 workers, the New Orleans District of the U.S. Army Corps of Engineers manages projects that provide navigation and flood control. The work of the Corps also protects and enhances the state's coastal and inland wetlands. These are not small tasks. The New Orleans District covers 30,000 square miles of south central and coastal Louisiana. Under the jurisdiction, or administration, of the Corps are 2,800 miles of navigable waterways, 950 miles of levees and floodwalls, 12 navigation **locks** (for raising and lowering boats between different water levels), and 6 major flood-control structures. Local levee districts are responsible for maintaining and repairing these structures, which are subject to hurricane and flood damage from time to time.

The Corps's New Orleans District also regulates dredge-and-fill operations in more than seven million acres of wetlands in the region. The process involves dredging, or removing the mud deposited by a river, and filling—or placing—it elsewhere. In addition, the district's expertise is needed to tackle hazardous and toxic-waste cleanup programs in support of the U.S. Environmental Protection Agency.

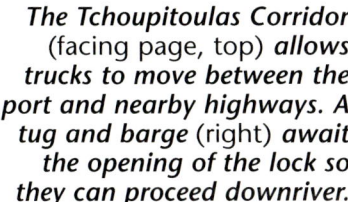

With the help of tugboats or towboats, flat-bottom barges (facing page, bottom) *move goods easily along inland rivers and waterways.*

Another outfit, the Eighth Coast Guard District, has several responsibilities along the Mississippi River and at the port. One of the Coast Guard's major duties is to maintain the red and green traffic signals on Algiers Point, a projection of land that sits directly across the river from the French Quarter.

The traffic lights regulate water traffic. During periods of high water, when ship pilots have difficulty steering their cumbersome vessels, freighters going upriver have to wait at the lights for southbound ships to get beyond Algiers Point. The signals let the pilots know when the shipping lanes are clear. Algiers Point bends almost 160 degrees, making it impossible for pilots to see around the tight corner. The lights warn pilots of approaching tugs, barges, and freighters, as does the radar system. Pilots are also connected by radio to the keeper of the traffic lights, who works onshore and can see when the lane is clear.

According to Louisiana law, all ships entering the Mississippi River must have a U.S. pilot on board. Pilots are certified masters, or captains, who steer the ship. A regular master, meanwhile, is responsible for the overall handling of the vessel. Pilots renew their licenses every five years. To demonstrate their knowledge of the river, pilots must pass a test and draw maps noting landmarks and obstacles.

The Coast Guard licenses river pilots to guide ships along certain sections of the Mississippi River. Some pilots qualify for several stretches of the river, while others concentrate only on one or two. For instance, one pilot can take a ship from the sea buoy in the Gulf of Mexico

> ▶ Over the centuries, the shape of the Mississippi River Delta has changed. Pass A L'Outre, South Pass, and Southwest Pass are the three main outlets to the Gulf. Southwest Pass is the deepest, allowing most freighter and barge traffic to travel easily.
>
> ▶ In early New Orleans, a broken levee was called a *crevasse*. A crevasse was a disaster. The explosion of water through the crack washed away everything in the water's path. Unless the levee was immediately repaired, it was almost impossible to get the river to return to its original course.
>
> ▶ On December 16, 1996, a 70,000-ton freighter lost power and rammed the Riverwalk Marketplace. The ship smashed into the mall after missing two passenger-filled cruise ships.

to Pilottown, Louisiana, just inside the mouth of the Mississippi. A second pilot guides the ship from Pilottown to New Orleans. Yet another pilot is then allowed to take the ship from New Orleans to Baton Rouge, Louisiana.

Specially licensed pilots guide ships around tricky curves, into narrow passages, and through the shallow waters of the lower Mississippi.

The Coast Guard's marine safety office ensures that each vessel carries approved life vests, life rafts, and other safety gear. A law-enforcement unit is used when police action is necessary. For example, sometimes police must search a ship for drugs or other illegal cargoes.

The U.S. Customs Service is a branch of the federal government that is responsible for the collection of duties, or import taxes, on products brought into the country. Customs agents assess the goods on ships and determine if they match those listed on the custom's application as well as those listed on the ship's manifest (the cargo list). Different products from different countries have different duty rates. It's the Customs Service's job to make sure that the correct duties are being collected. In addition, customs agents work to prevent the import of illegal products, such as drugs.

New Orleans is a leading U.S. port. It receives cargo from as far away as Minnesota, Colorado, and Pennsylvania. In fact, port promoters emphasize that New Orleans acts as Middle America's port. The facilities at the Port of New Orleans offer 22 million square feet of cargo storage area, plus 7.5 million square feet of covered storage area to accommodate a total of more than 30 million tons of cargo each year.

◄ **Nearby Port Facilities**

But New Orleans is not the only port facility on the lower Mississippi River. Several nearby communities also handle raw materials and finished goods for the international market. The lower Mississippi is always bustling with incoming and outgoing vessels. Docks, warehouses, factories, storage tanks, and offices stretch for miles along both banks of the mud-brown river.

The Port of South Louisiana (PSL) sits midway between New Orleans and Baton Rouge. More tonnage moves through PSL's jurisdiction than in any port region in the United States. PSL's 205-acre Globalplex Intermodal Terminal has docking both for low, clunky barges and for sleek oceangoing ships. This allows the terminal to take in almost any type of cargo, including wood chips, limestone, natural gas, steel beams, chemicals, animal fats, and hefty bags of rice. The port is also the terminus, or endpoint, for 500,000 barrels of oil delivered daily

Pipes bring crude oil that has been pumped out of oil fields in the Gulf of Mexico to a storage facility in Louisiana.

from underwater oil-producing fields 15 miles out in the Gulf of Mexico. The oil gurgles through a 48-inch-wide pipe that snakes inland to the terminal's huge, round storage tanks. A 40-inch-wide, 640-mile-long pipeline then carries 800,000 barrels of oil daily from Louisiana to sites throughout the Midwest.

PSL is linked to the rest of the country by Interstate Highways 10, 55, and 59, as well as by the Kansas City Southern and Illinois Central Railroads. These bustling transportation links allow goods to move speedily in and out of the port to and from regions of the United States, Canada, Mexico, and South America.

PSL's Globalplex facility is more than just a port. It's a prime industrial site. A purification plant treats seven million gallons of water per day. A waste-treatment facility also handles 250,000 gallons of sewage daily. Sugar and oil refineries, fertilizer and chemical plants, grain elevators, and a steel-processing factory are located on another 50,000 acres of land administered by the port.

The Domino Sugar factory refines imported raw sugar and prepares it for redistribution throughout the United States.

An oil refinery turns crude oil from the Gulf of Mexico into useable fuel.

The Port of St. Bernard is a few miles downriver from New Orleans. In addition to its prime waterfront location, it also directs operations at the nearby Arabi Terminal and Industrial Park. The Port of St. Bernard focuses on serving the textile industry. This type of operation, called a niche, concentrates on only one type of good. Apparel, or clothing, is made at St. Bernard and transported in and out of the port. The port handles both the shipping and receiving of raw materials and finished goods.

Local manufacturing plants cut the cloth, which is then sent overseas for sewing. The finished clothing is returned to the port for land distribution. Freight forwarders, customs brokers, trucking firms, railway lines, and shipping officials work closely together. They want to be sure that the latest fashions are quickly produced and delivered to department stores. The port's main markets are in Mexico, the western Caribbean, and Central and South America, as well as throughout the United States.

CHAPTER TWO

HISTORIC NEW ORLEANS

Spanish moss drips from trees in the Barataria Swamp (facing page), *one of many places where, for hundreds of years, Native Americans hunted and fished.*

The wilderness of the Mississippi River Delta was long a hospitable home for the Choctaw, Biloxi, Bayougoula, and Mougoulacha Native American nations. They lived along the shadowy bayous and ventured where the cypress groves were so thick the trees cut off much of the sun. Families adjusted to the soaring heat and humidity by living in reed houses that let in the breeze. They slept in hammocks if it was too warm inside their homes.

The Native Americans lived off the land as skilled hunters and fishers, trapping otter and muskrats and catching abundant fish. They survived in the swampy region, in spite of the presence of giant alligators and poisonous snakes called water moccasins. In fact, the Mississippi River and its delta were central to the Indians' lives. The Indians' boats glided easily and swiftly along the river to the Gulf of Mexico, where they collected shells and caught fish along the shoreline. They grew vegetables in the rich soil deposited by the river.

The mouth of the Mississippi was a prime crossroads for trade among many cultures. Native Americans from other parts of the North American continent journeyed down the river or along the Gulf Coast to trade with local peoples. Villagers traveled up the Mississippi far to the north, west, and east in search of goods. Some historians believe these trade routes reached as far north as Minnesota and southward deep into Mexico. These commercial connections may have extended to Caribbean islands and to Central and South America.

Tribes in present-day Louisiana traded furs, blankets, pottery, baskets, and other items for food and other goods that could not be grown or found in the delta country. Pearls and valuable quartz crystals were used as currency between the various Native American nations. For centuries before the arrival of Europeans, commerce was an important aspect of living in Mississippi delta country.

◀ **Newcomers Arrive**

In the 1500s, Europeans became fascinated with the idea that there might be a river crossing North America. They hoped it would be a passage from the Atlantic to the Pacific Oceans. That dream led many an explorer up and down the great Mississippi. One of the first Europeans to see the river was the Spanish adventurer and gold seeker, Hernando de Soto.

In May 1541, de Soto crossed the river somewhere north of the area that eventually became Louisiana. He wrote in his diary that the river was full of logs and very muddy. De Soto died of fever shortly after making the crossing, and his weighted body was tossed into the water for burial. His exploration team headed downstream, passing the site of what would become New Orleans, and continued on to the Gulf.

Because de Soto's expedition team found no gold during its travels through the Mississippi River Valley, Spain lost interest in the region. For well over 100 years, Europeans stayed away. In 1673 the French explorers Louis Joliet and Father Jacques Marquette paddled down the Mississippi as far south as the Arkansas River, turning back because of hostile encounters with Native Americans.

In the 1600s, Father Jacques Marquette and Louis Joliet traveled down the Mississippi with the help of their Native American guides.

About 10 years later, the French explorer Sieur René-Robert Cavelier de La Salle, traveled all the way down the Mississippi to the Gulf. He was seeking a water route for exporting furs from North America to Europe. La Salle put up a cross on the riverbank in April 1682, claiming all the land drained by the river for the king of France. La Salle named the entire region Louisiana in honor of King Louis XIV.

The first European colony in the territory was established more than a decade later. Pierre Le Moyne, Sieur d'Iberville, and his brother Jean-Baptiste Le Moyne, Sieur de Bienville, led a party of French colonists to the Gulf of Mexico. They reached the Gulf Coast in 1699 on the Tuesday before the Christian holiday of Ash Wednesday. That day happened to be the feast of Mardi Gras, which launches the Catholic fasting season of Lent. D'Iberville named his camp Mardi Gras in honor of the holy day. As the explorers set up camp, Indians came over and showed the latest group of French arrivals some prayer books and a letter left behind by La Salle's party. These materials assured D'Iberville that he had found the right river.

Over the next few years, the French colonists (settlers) built forts along the Gulf Coast. More people arrived from France. Some were convicts, vagrants, and other unfortunates who were faced with the hard choice of going to the Bastille—the toughest prison in France—or of coming to the North American wilderness.

A Scottish financier named John Law established Natchitoches, the first permanent European settlement in Louisiana, in 1714. The

The French explorer Sieur René-Robert Cavalier de La Salle, raised a cross near the mouth of the Mississippi several days after claiming the territory. He named the area Louisiana, after the French king Louis XIV.

◀ **First Settlements**

French king gave Law permission to recruit colonists for Louisiana. Law's agents scoured Europe looking for people brave enough or foolish enough to depart for the unknown continent. They were promised vast riches, tracts of land, and an easy life. In reality many new arrivals found only disease and hard work.

To attract settlers to the newly established Louisiana settlement, John Law had this "advertisement" made to show the wealth and luxurious lifestyle of the new port city. However, many newcomers found life in Natchitoches very hard.

In 1717 Bienville was named governor of Louisiana. The colony of Louisiana was far larger than the current state is. The colony was bordered by the Mississippi River Basin, which extended from the Appalachian Mountains to the Rocky Mountains and from Canada to the Gulf of Mexico. A year later, Bienville explored the land surrounding a Native American village called Tchoutchouma. This village was near a

33

portage (overland route) between the Mississippi River and Lake Pontchartrain. Bienville decided this village would be the best place for a port city. Its location at a bend in the deep, wide river was perfect. The site was far enough from the Gulf so sandbars and storms would not be a problem, yet it was situated where ships could easily dock.

Bienville and his friend John Law figured that at this location goods could be unloaded from ships coming downriver. The cargo would then be carried overland and reloaded on vessels berthed at Lake Pontchartrain. Indians had shown Bienville that the quickest route to Biloxi and Mobile—the other colonial villages along the Gulf—was by way of the portage to Lake Pontchartrain rather than by the river. The lake was connected to the Gulf via the Rigolets, a series of sluggish streams. In 1718 Bienville named the city he founded New Orleans after the duke of Orleans, the regent who ruled France until young King Louis XV reached maturity.

Because so much of the area surrounding New Orleans lay below sea level, Native Americans showed the settlers how to find high, dry ground on which to build shelters. The Indians taught the Europeans to grow pumpkins, rice, and beans.

As more settlers came, the city grew. In 1722 developers drafted a plan for the city. The plan marked streets in a grid pattern, instead of the hodgepodge, random development of the early days. This settlement is known as the French Quarter, or Vieux Carré (old square), because of its grid configuration.

In its early years, New Orleans was surrounded by sugarcane plantations. These large farms were in the *faubourgs,* or suburbs, of the city. But as New Orleans expanded, the plantations were absorbed into the city. In 1737 New Orleans became a crown colony, a change that put it directly under the control of its local government—not of faraway France.

Political Changes

In 1762 the Seven Years' War (called the French and Indian War in what became the United States) was ending. France was one of the losers. As a result, France transferred to Spain control of the Louisiana colony west of the Mississippi and south of Lake Pontchartrain. (The eastern section of Louisiana extending from the Appalachians to the Mississippi and south to Lake Pontchartrain went to Britain.) Many of New Orleans's original French settlers objected to Spanish rule and revolted. The Spanish sent a new administrator named Alejandro O'Reilly to put down the rebellion. Residents gave him the nickname "Bloody O'Reilly" for the methods he used to squelch the uprising.

Despite the political changes happening in North America, farmers surged into the valley near the Ohio River throughout the 1770s. When they harvested their crops, they had difficulty shipping them eastward, where British merchants lived. So the farmers began shipping their products down the Ohio and Mississippi Rivers to New Orleans. At this time, Britain—which controlled eastern North America—was feuding with Spain. Although it was illegal for these British (and soon-to-be American)

In the late 1700s, the Spanish government sent Alejandro O'Reilly to Louisiana to calm local objection to Spanish rule. The people of the port came to call him "Bloody O'Reilly" for his harsh treatment.

citizens to trade with Spanish Louisiana, they needed one another.

During the American Revolution (1775–1783), Spanish troops from Louisiana aided the American colonists in their quest for freedom from British control. The Spaniards guarded the Gulf Coast and Florida against British attack. Spanish efforts helped the colonists win independence.

In 1795 Spain and the newly formed United States of America signed a treaty that established legal, two-way **trade concessions,** or trading rights, that offered economic advantages to both countries. The treaty helped New Orleans become a major port and strengthened an interdependent relationship between the U.S. citizens of the Ohio Valley and the colonists in Spanish Louisiana.

The harbor bustled with activity as eager newcomers poured in from around the world. Among the immigrants were thousands of refugees fleeing a slave uprising on St. Domingue (modern Haiti). Along with the white refugees were many ex-slaves who were skilled craftworkers, painters, writers, and performers. Their creative talents helped make New Orleans one of the most cultured communities in the Americas.

The city was also among the wealthiest in North America, as river and Gulf trade increased. Cotton, rice, sugar, rum, and tobacco were among the principal commodities transported from New Orleans to other markets. Flatboats loaded with materials such as flour, whiskey, and timber drifted down the Mississippi from northern ports. Sailing vessels from

> ▶ Colonial New Orleans had one of the largest slave markets in North America. The city's first census in 1720 counted 14 white men, 65 white women, 38 white children, 172 African slaves, and 21 Indian slaves.
>
> ▶ Fires in 1788 and 1794 destroyed many French-built structures in the city of New Orleans. These buildings were replaced with new ones of Spanish design. Thus the historic French Quarter looks more Spanish than French.

overseas docked at wharves lining the New Orleans riverfront. Yet there were problems. Although New Orleans was thousands of miles from Europe, it was affected by political affairs far across the Atlantic.

The Louisiana Purchase

The Spanish governor of Louisiana had helped the Americans during the American Revolution by attacking British forts and diverting British troops. The Americans were happy to have Spanish-held Louisiana as a neighbor.

Although France and Spain had long had a rocky relationship, they shared one thing: a mutual distrust of the British. Napoléon Bonaparte came to power in France in 1799. He began dreaming of reestablishing France as a great colonial power in the profitable Caribbean islands and in continental North America. In 1800 he negotiated with Spain to return Louisiana to France. To save the cost of administering the colony, Spain agreed to the proposal. In October 1801, both parties ratified the Treaty of San Ildefonso in secret. Spain, however, remained the ruler of Louisiana for the next three years.

Napoléon's plans to build a new empire in Louisiana crumbled when his troops stopped in St. Domingue. The island was experiencing an epidemic of yellow fever and a slave rebellion. Both events reduced the army's numbers. Napoléon decided to delay his plans for Louisiana and to concentrate instead on declaring war on Britain.

U.S. president Thomas Jefferson was disturbed by rumors that France was the new owner of Louisiana and that Britain also had its

Napoléon Bonaparte

eye on the colony. He told Robert Livingston, America's minister to France, to try to buy the Isle of Orleans (the strip of land between the river, the lake, and the Gulf) and the two Floridas (East and West). The United States was willing to pay $2 million, which was 20 percent of its treasury, for this small, 2,800-square-mile area. At first, the French seemed uninterested. Then the French foreign minister startled Livingston by asking if the United States would be interested in buying the whole of Louisiana. Livingston stalled by saying that he didn't have the authority to go beyond his original orders.

This new proposal—to sell the whole, huge colony of Louisiana—came directly from Napoléon himself. He had neither the funds nor a strong navy to protect the distant colony. And he preferred that a weak United States, rather than a powerful Britain, possess the region.

The total tab was $15 million for 828,000 square miles. The deal, called the Louisiana Purchase, peacefully doubled the size of the United States. Neither the French nor the Americans knew the exact boundaries of this area. Nevertheless, the agreement was signed in May 1803.

Several months were spent on planning the transfer of the colony from Spain to France and then from France to the United States. On November 30, 1803, the Spanish flag was lowered and the French flag hoisted in the public square in front of St. Louis Cathedral. On December 20, the French formally handed over the vast colony to U.S. representatives.

What was the impact of the Louisiana Purchase? The United States obtained control of the Mississippi River for trade via the Port of New Orleans. Thirteen states or parts of states were eventually carved from the original colony. The purchase caused settlers to surge into the new territory and to begin the westward expansion of the United States. And it was all because the United States knew its destiny depended on the Port of New Orleans as its outlet for the Mississippi River. No other port in the country can claim such an impact on American history.

Growth and Change ▶ U.S. citizens flooded into New Orleans, looking for new opportunities. At first the old-timers objected to the newcomers. The original inhabitants of the city were mostly Catholics who spoke French and were accustomed to French laws. The newcomers were different. Many were Protestant. They spoke English. Many

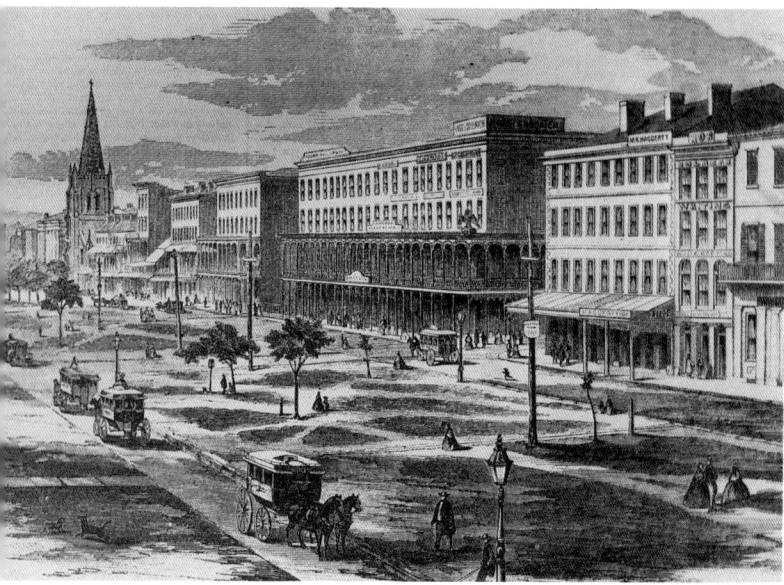

Canal Street was the neutral ground where English-speaking newcomers and ancestors of the French settlers could conduct business without fear of fights breaking out.

fights occurred between the two cultures. Duels were held under the oaks in City Park. For a time, it seemed that these differences would never be resolved.

Canal Street was a dividing line between the newcomers and the early settlers, or Creoles, who lived in the French Quarter. The 90-foot-wide median in the center of the street was called a neutral ground. This area was where business transactions between the two groups could be conducted safely. Eventually, all median strips in the city became known as neutral grounds, a term that is still used.

Two events solidified the destiny of New Orleans. In January 1812, the *New Orleans* became the first steamboat to arrive in the city, having traveled four months downriver from Pittsburgh, Pennsylvania. Then, in April, Louisiana became the eighteenth state to join the Union.

The first steamboat to arrive in New Orleans made its maiden voyage down the Mississippi River from Pittsburgh, Pennsylvania. The **New Orleans** *arrived in New Orleans on January 10, 1812. Steamboats have been a familiar sight on the river ever since.*

Both events opened up fantastic new trade possibilities for the port city.

But New Orleans was still influenced by what went on far from its lively social and commercial scene. Since 1793 France and Britain had been at war. The United States tried to stay neutral, but both European countries seized American ships on the high seas. The U.S. Congress passed the Embargo Act in 1807, cutting off trade with both Britain and France. This policy dealt a harsh blow to New Orleans's economy. Business was cut by one-third, and many people were forced into bankruptcy.

After several American sailors were forced to serve in the British navy, the United States declared war on Britain in June 1812. Three years later, U.S. and British soldiers fought the last battle of the war just outside New Orleans. The U.S. Army, led by General Andrew Jackson, beat the British troops. Pirates, ex-slaves, Kentucky sharpshooters, and Creoles made up most of the American force. They were joined by people of

U.S. general Andrew Jackson (on white horse), *head of the military government in New Orleans, defeated the British army in the final battle of the War of 1812.*

many nationalities who had found homes and economic opportunities in New Orleans.

This motley force was fighting to protect the largest city west of the Appalachian Mountains. After the war, the city's economy and port boomed. Natural resources from the country's inland markets were unloaded at the port to be put on ships going overseas. Heading back upriver, the steamboats carried all sorts of manufactured products, from lead pipes to furniture.

Even a terrible yellow fever epidemic in 1853 did not slow down the engines of commerce. The disease was brought to New Orleans on Jamaican ships whose water barrels were infested with mosquito larva. (The dreaded disease is carried by mosquitoes, a fact not discovered until almost 100 years later.)

War and Rebirth

When the Civil War broke out in 1861 between the North (the Union) and the South (the Confederacy), New Orleans was the largest city in

▶ Creoles, or people of French or Spanish heritage born in the Louisiana colony, dominated the city's economic life in the late 1700s and early 1800s. Most Creoles had kept strong ties to France. But some Creoles had African ancestors who'd been brought to the colony as slaves. These African-descended Creoles worked the vast plantations of the region.

the South and one of the world's major cotton markets. Steamboats calling at New Orleans brought in hundreds of millions of dollars worth of trade. The ships annually hauled two million bales of cotton from southern plantations to mills in New England.

The city's strategic location on the Mississippi River and its great wealth meant that to win the war the Union needed to control the city.

Two men help bury the bodies of the many people who died in 1853 of yellow fever. Studies later discovered that mosquitoes had carried the deadly disease.

U.S. naval forces, led by Admiral William Farragut, captured Confederate forts along the river in the second Battle of New Orleans. After these defenses were gone, New Orleans quickly

fell. From 1862 to 1877, during and after the war, New Orleans was under the tight control of U.S. troops. These years were a bitter time for the Confederate sympathizers who lived in the once-bustling port.

After the Union won the war in 1865, the United States continued to expand westward. But the fighting had destroyed railroads and steamboats in the South. Passes down the Mississippi River were silted up, and little cargo arrived in the Port of New Orleans. As a result, railroads bypassed New Orleans and laid their rails east to west rather than north to south. Trains called at St. Louis, Missouri, and Chicago, Illinois, instead of at New Orleans. The economy of the port suffered.

But New Orleans's advantageous position on the Mississippi River and the port's proximity to the Gulf were still considered desirable for transporting international goods, especially from South and Central America. Railroads eventually aimed southward to pick up coffee and bananas shipped to New Orleans from Latin America. The railroad traffic helped New Orleans rebound economically at the end of the 1800s.

As the port continued to grow and prosper, Louisiana politicians and businesspeople realized that the port was the city's principal means of income. In 1896 the Louisiana legislature formed the powerful Board of Commissioners of the Port of New Orleans. What was good for New Orleans, they reasoned, was good for Louisiana. The Board of Commissioners, also known as the Dock Board, held authority over

Early on in the Civil War (1861–1865), New Orleans fell quickly to the forces of the Union Army (facing page). *During the conflict, the city's economy suffered. But by the end of the 1800s, New Orleans had rebuilt much of the port. The city was back in business, and the port was booming* (below).

In 1920 dock workers pose in front of the first building of the Dock Board (established 1896).

all the waterfront in Orleans **Parish** and much of the waterfront in adjoining St. Bernard and Jefferson Parishes.

In 1901 the Dock Board tore down out-of-date warehouses and rebuilt much of the New Orleans waterfront. Within a decade, the port became a modern, efficient facility with state-of-the-art cotton- and grain-storage facilities. Blocks of new warehouses lined the river.

The Levee Board of New Orleans oversaw the dikes along the river and Lake Pontchartrain. In 1924 the board unveiled a plan to build higher levees, to transform the lake bottom into new subdivisions, and to create new beaches, parks, and other attractions. Workers constructed a 5.5-mile-long protective seawall 3,000 feet into the lake. Muck from the lake bottom was pumped into the space between the seawall and the shore. The landfill added another 2,000 acres to the city. For the first time in 200 years, most of the city's flood problems were resolved. Subdivisions sprang up where once there had been swamps.

> ▶ In old New Orleans, wooden sidewalks called *banquettes* were built three feet above the street surface because the roads were under water so often. Rain, however, can still be a problem. The low-lying streets flood during especially heavy downpours, and shopowners often put sandbags around their doors to keep out the water.
>
> ▶ New Orleans's first bridges over the Mississippi were built in the 1950s. Until then ferry boats packed with people and cargo crossed the river.

A DEADLY CANAL

In the late 1980s, road workers in New Orleans uncovered a mass grave of several hundred men. The shocking find reminded citizens of the suffering earlier inhabitants had endured to build their city, especially the New Basin Canal.

Designed to bring cargo from Lake Pontchartrain to the city center, the freight canal was to be large enough to accommodate heavy barges. A wide basin, or pool, allowed these shallow-draft ships to turn around for the return trip across the lake.

In the 1830s, thousands of Irish and German immigrants were recruited to dig the six-mile-long canal. The immigrants lived with hot, humid temperatures, disease, back-breaking labor, and low wages. Everything was done by hand. No steam shovels or bulldozers existed to make the task easier. Diggers had to use picks and shovels.

The work conditions took their toll on crews. Anyone who died was rolled into the mud and buried on the spot. If a mud slide occurred, the work continued around the trapped men, who were often abandoned to die. More than 8,000 workers died of injuries or illness while building the New Basin Canal.

Those who survived, however, became the backbone of New Orleans's port economy. They took jobs on the docks, such as packing cotton in the holds of steamboats or working in warehouses. Many joined the police and fire departments. Others became business owners, educators, lawyers, mayors, and legislators.

By 1961 the turning spot for the ships had become the site of the city's train and bus depot. But the dead weren't forgotten. In 1990 the Irish Cultural Society of New Orleans put up a cross at the canal in memory of the laborers who had lost their lives constructing it.

Modern Times

Upgrading and maintaining port facilities is never-ending work. Ports around the world remain competitive in the international shipping trade by having the most up-to-date facilities for their customers. A worldwide cargo transportation revolution began in the 1960s with the introduction of **containerization.** Previously, cargo had to be loaded and unloaded multiple times between leaving the manufacturing plant and arriving at the buyer's door. The new concept was to load cargo into a metal box that was detachable from the truck or rail chassis (frame). The box, called a container, can be quickly and inexpensively moved from truck or train to ship. Eliminating the additional handling cuts labor costs. In addition, there is less loss from theft or damage, and the container moves much more rapidly from point of origin to destination.

In the late 1960s, the Port of New Orleans decided to develop special container facilities to handle **intermodal transportation,** in which cargo can be transferred from road, to rail, to ship. Several years later, in 1973, officials dedicated the port's first container berth as part of a 30-year, $400 million development plan.

Wharf upgrades continued throughout the remainder of the decade and into the 1980s. The port built container docks along the Industrial Canal, which lay closer to the interstate highway system and a shorter distance from the Gulf than the old docks. Five wharves along the river were also rebuilt. Meanwhile, developers converted many warehouses in the former downtown riverfront port area into nightclubs, museums, art galleries, and restaurants.

Laborers use special cranes to load and unload containerized cargo.

The Industrial Canal was completed in 1923. It was one of the early projects undertaken by the Dock Board in 1916.

New plans put up office buildings where old, worn-out structures had once stood. Modern construction techniques anchored the new buildings' tall steel skeletons to solid bedrock hidden far below the watery surface.

By the 1990s, however, the wharves along the Industrial Canal were beginning to show their limitations. Larger ship designs required a deeper draft, or water depth, than the canal could provide. The possibility of deepening the canal seemed uncertain, so port officials decided to keep their primary operations in the upper riverfront area.

A $215 million renovation started in 1990 made the port one of the nation's most modern shipping and storage facilities. The new docks built between 1990 and 1996 are located in the uptown area close to the western branch of the Gulf Intracoastal Waterway, which brings additional traffic to the port. This waterway allows barge tows to travel east from the Rio Grande in Texas to the Florida coast without having to battle the rough waters of the Gulf of Mexico. The Port of New Orleans continues to make adjustments to ensure viability into the twenty-first century.

CHAPTER THREE

THE PORT AT WORK

A container ship docks at the France Road Wharf (facing page) *along the banks of the Industrial Canal.*

The Port of New Orleans is one of the busiest in the world. More than 30 million tons of cargo enter and leave the public and private terminals each year. The port handles an average of 2,400 vessels annually. Colorful flags from dozens of countries fly from the forest of masts along the docks.

The port provides jobs to many people in New Orleans. More than 51,000 people work on the 22 miles of wharves and terminals on the Mississippi River, the container ship facilities along the Industrial Canal, and along the Mississippi River–Gulf Outlet. One of every 12 jobs in New Orleans has links to the port. Laborers unload ships, secretaries work in freight-company offices, and grain-elevator operators, security guards, and shipping personnel all keep the port bustling with activity.

These jobs are part of the wide variety of businesses headquartered at the port. The shipyards of New Orleans, for example, have long been a major Louisiana business. In the mid-1990s, Avondale Shipyards was the largest private employer in the state, with 6,000 workers on its payroll. Located five miles upriver from the New Orleans business district, Avondale ranks among the nation's top five shipbuilders. The company's biggest customer is the U.S. Navy.

Avondale builds powerful minesweepers (warships designed to neutralize mines), as well as 950-foot-long transports (used to move troops and supplies). These ships are not small-ticket items. A navy oil tanker, for example,

▶ The New Orleans port facilities are worth $700 million. This figure includes the value of 22 million square feet of cargo handling space and 7.5 million square feet of covered storage.

▶ Port-related businesses spend an estimated $11.4 billion throughout Louisiana.

▶ Metrowide, the port generates more than 50,000 jobs, $6 billion in total spending, and $261.7 million in state and local tax revenue.

Facilities of the Avondale Shipyards—including two dry docks, a 200-ton gantry crane, and a 628-ton floating crane bridge—repair and upgrade a wide variety of ships.

These storage facilities at Silocaf of New Orleans replaced the 73-year-old New Orleans Public Grain Elevator in 1993. The processing plant is the world's largest facility for processing green (raw) coffee beans.

costs upward of $100 million dollars to construct. Like many New Orleans firms, Avondale seeks more clients as the U.S. military budget for new ships decreases. For the domestic market, the shipyard builds new vessels and refurbishes tankers to meet the regulations of the Oil Pollution Act of 1990. This law specifies that any ship cruising U.S. waters must have two hulls to help limit oil leakage in case of an accident.

The port is also home to Silocaf of New Orleans, the world's largest bulk green (raw) coffee storage facility. Based at the Nashville Avenue

terminal, the Italian-owned company handles 274,000 tons of raw coffee beans each year. Beans from Brazil, Colombia, El Salvador, Mexico, and Guatemala are unloaded and hauled to the company's New Orleans processing plant.

In recent years, the Port of New Orleans has seen increases in coffee imports, especially from Latin American countries.

Farther downriver a sprawling facility transforms raw brown sugar from Louisiana and Latin America into white refined sugar to be shipped to domestic markets. Each day Domino Sugar processes 6.2 million pounds of sugar. The sweet stuff is sent out in packets, 5-pound bags, 55-pound bags, or by the barge load.

A substantial military presence exists alongside the commercial ventures at the port. New Orleans historically has been a strategic military center. Since its founding, the city has been a garrison town. During World War II, landing craft for the D day invasion of Europe were built in the Higgins Ship Yards and sent overseas. More recently equipment destined for the 1991 Desert Storm action against Iraq was shipped through New Orleans. Personnel carriers, tanks, and other armored vehicles were lined up in neat rows along the wharves, ready to be sent to the Middle East. According to port officials, about $3-billion worth of military goods move annually through the Port of New Orleans.

Trading Goods More than 123,000 people in the New Orleans region can trace their jobs directly or indirectly to international trade. About 22 percent of the regional economy depends on waterborne commerce. This means shipping is big, big business in New Orleans.

Grain and petroleum products comprise most of the shipments out of the port. Each day drilling rigs in the Gulf of Mexico pump hundreds of thousands of gallons of crude oil from

A plant in New Orleans constructs offshore drilling platforms. When completed, the oil rigs will stand on the seafloor of the Gulf of Mexico, where they will take their turns pumping petroleum to the surface.

under the surface. The oil is piped inland to refineries near New Orleans. Along with crude petroleum imported from Latin America and the Middle East, domestic crude is carried aboard bulky tankers.

The fertile soil of North Dakota, South Dakota, Minnesota, Iowa, Illinois, and Missouri produces millions of tons of grain each year. During the harvest, farmers in these states haul their rich bounty to grain elevators for storage. Trains and trucks then bring the produce to major ports along the Mississippi River, where the grain is transferred to low-slung barges for the long journey to the Crescent City. Corn, soybeans, and wheat travel southward on heavily laden barges. The bulky cargo carriers are pushed along the Mississippi River by snorting tugboats.

Steel and steel products are imported and exported through New Orleans. Steel pipes and beams, rolled steel, sheet steel, and machinery

After goods arrive in New Orleans, barges (below), *trucks, and trains transport them inland.*

made in the United States and Japan cross the wharves. Some products come from mills in Chicago and from Gary, Indiana. Giant steel bulldozers and tractors made in Peoria, Illinois, are shipped downriver for eventual sale in Latin America.

Metal alloys (mixtures) and various grades of steel come to New Orleans from around the world. Tons of steel pour in from Japan, Finland, and Brazil. Mountains of aluminum from Russia rise atop the wharves. Towers of copper

Imports to the Port of New Orleans include steel products (above), *hardwoods* (right), *and copper* (below). *In the mid-1990s, steel made up the largest volume of cargo shipped through the Port of New Orleans.*

from Chile and Peru fill the sheds. The raw materials are destined for manufacturing plants throughout the United States. Products made from these substances may be sent back to international markets through the Port of New Orleans.

Ships take giant rolls of linerboard, made from Louisiana pine, to China to be made into boxes and cartons. Workers stack mahogany lumber from Bolivia outside the sheds, while endless rows of plywood sheets from Indonesia,

Malaysia, and Thailand crowd the sheds' interiors.

Raw coffee beans come in from Latin America, Africa, and Asia to be roasted into the rich, dark flavor that coffee drinkers love. The Port of New Orleans is the top coffee-handling port in the United States. Midwestern soybeans leave the port for worldwide markets. Nutritious agricultural products from Arkansas go out. Barges bring raw rubber from Indonesia to tire factories in the northern United States. The huge tires end up in underground mines in Chile and Peru.

Global Markets

New Orleans is like a revolving door—a city tied to the global market, in part through trade incentives such as the **North American Free Trade Agreement (NAFTA).** This trade

agreement economically links Canada, the United States, and Mexico, allowing goods to pass freely from country to country without duties.

Some politicians complain about such treaties and want to set up trade barriers to keep foreign goods out of the United States. Called **protectionism,** this theory argues that trade barriers protect America's standard of living by ensuring that citizens purchase goods made in the United States. Higher American wages mean that U.S.-made products often cost more than do foreign products from nations that pay low wages. Nevertheless, protectionists believe buying American is the essence of a strong economy. Other lawmakers believe that being connected to the rest of the world is the root of a healthy national economy. Consumers overseas become more important as their national economies grow stronger and as they have more money to buy U.S. goods. If the United States blocks goods and products from entering its borders, other nations could fight back by preventing American materials from being sold in their homelands.

By staying abreast of technological innovations and changes in the global economy, the Port of New Orleans has been able to remain competitive. It has excellent transportation links to ensure that goods are received and delivered safely and promptly. New Orleans can often offer better inland freight rates to the domestic market than competing port cities can.

President Bill Clinton signed the North American Free Trade Agreement (facing page) *in 1994. The agreement, which strengthens trade with Mexico, may increase shipping in the Port of New Orleans. The port's own efforts to foster trade with Latin America may also boost commercial traffic.*

The Latin Link ▶ In addition, New Orleans is closer to Latin America than some of its competitors are, making shipping less expensive. New Orleans has long-standing business contacts with Latin America, especially Central America. And Latin America is an important growth area for commerce into and out of New Orleans. In recent years, the highest growth rates in trade have been with Argentina, Brazil, Chile, Costa Rica, Ecuador, El Salvador, Guatemala, Honduras, Panama, and Peru.

The New Orleans port works closely with local officials in arranging trade missions and in organizing seminars on Latin American commerce. Each year the city hosts Encuentro, a trade exposition for U.S. and Latin American businesses. Delegates compare notes, look over exhibits, and plan how to increase trade between North, Central, and South America.

MetroVision—a partnership of New Orleans's business, labor, governmental, educational, and civic organizations—coordinates the marketing and promotion for the lower section of the Mississippi River to ensure it remains economically strong. The group's mission, to create jobs in the region around the city, is accomplished in part with a plan called InterCambio 2000.

MetroVision hopes to boost the port's economy by serving the growing markets along the Gulf Coasts of Mexico and Central America and along the western coast of South America. Target industries are oil and gas equipment and services—the materials necessary for oil exploration and production. The organization hopes that by attracting better airline service, adding more manufacturing, and boosting general port capabilities, international trade can pump

▶ Until World War II, New Orleans dominated trade between the United States and Latin America. But in the 1950s, Miami and Houston emerged as strong competitors for New Orleans. The Port of New Orleans set out to regain its lead. By the mid-1990s, the New Orleans customs district was second to Miami and ahead of Houston in trade with Latin American countries.

▶ Trade creates new jobs. According to MetroVision, 5,100 more jobs result from every $1 billion of new trade handled by the ports in the New Orleans region.

another $2 billion into the area's economy. Some planners predict that more than 10,000 new jobs may be created as a result of Metro-Vision's work.

In addition to oil and gas machinery, the InterCambio 2000 plan has earmarked six additional core industries that have the best potential for overseas trade. They include agricultural chemicals, processed foods, pollution-control equipment, hotel and restaurant equipment, and medical equipment. Travel and tourism are also key factors in the growth plan.

Many organizations work hard to ensure that the Port of New Orleans remains strong and continues to grow. Although the future is difficult to predict, port marketing experts have a sense of the future of global business. They consider which countries might be potential growth markets, and then ask: What U.S. goods do these countries need? How can New Orleans service other nations? They also look at business from the American side. What do U.S. firms require to stay competitive? Can they use a new product from overseas? How can the port accommodate American companies?

Here is an example of how the Port of New Orleans capitalized on an opportunity. In recent decades, Americans have become increasingly health conscious. Red meat became a no-no, and everyone was singing the praises of poultry, especially the white meat from chicken and turkeys. The demand for chicken breasts soared. But since a chicken also is part dark meat, what can you do with the millions of chicken legs and thighs that no one is buying? Try to find a new market.

HOT STUFF

Have you ever taken a bite of a spicy food and thought your breath could light a match? Think of what 500 to 800 *tons* of fiery sauce could do! That much Crystal Hot Sauce is shipped worldwide from the Port of New Orleans each month. Crystal International Corporation, a division of Baumer Foods Incorporated, produces the hot stuff for international consumption.

Workers have been making mouth-blazing Crystal Hot Sauce in New Orleans since 1923. The stuff's ingredients consist of cayenne peppers mixed with vinegar and salt. Crystal Hot Sauce can be used on anything from meat to eggs—and on anything else if you like. The spicy sauce is an essential ingredient in many Creole dishes. Creole dishes most often contain okra, rice, tomatoes, peppers, and meat or seafood.

The company packages most Crystal Hot Sauce in glass containers for shipping and eventual overseas sales. Workers put a gallon size in plastic, like a jug of milk. The company also ships the sauce in 55-gallon drums to other manufacturers. As an extra service, Crystal often labels the jars and cans printed in the language of the importing country. To send its product overseas, Crystal puts the cases of sauce into containers that are placed in the ship's hold. Sometimes cases are stacked on pallets and lifted by a crane.

The sauce's red color and spicy taste may remind you of fire engines, but Crystal thinks more about ships. Freighters carry the firm's mouth-steaming product to 75 countries around the world. The greatest volume of sauce goes to Middle Eastern nations such as Saudi Arabia. The people there love the flavorful mixture on their food, just as much as Louisianans do. With three million cases of Crystal Hot Sauce flowing through the Port of New Orleans a year, you can bet it adds spice to port life!

The port's marketing department worked with its poultry customers from Arkansas, Mississippi, and Louisiana and with local cold-storage warehouses to try to find likely customers that could be served from the Port of New Orleans. Their research paid off when they discovered that Russians and other citizens of the former Soviet bloc were hungry for fresh meat and had the money to buy it. So a team of port, poultry, and maritime officials traveled to eastern Europe to pitch dark-meat poultry products. The Russians flocked to buy the tasty birds. And the money the poultry companies, port, steamship lines, warehouse people, and longshore workers earned wasn't chicken feed!

As a matter of course, the port's maritime team also worked on finding valuable return cargoes. Soon thousands of tons of eastern European steel and aluminum were pouring

In 1996 the Board of Commissioners of the Port of New Orleans (formerly the Dock Board) celebrated its centennial anniversary. This office building is the new site for the Port Commission.

A ship from one of the 70 steamship lines that service the Port of New Orleans heads for its berth. Six rail lines, 75 truck lines, and 16 barge lines also make stops at the port.

into New Orleans's wharves, generating lots of jobs from the docks to the Midwest.

By paying attention to international business news and by listening to consumers, the port captured a profitable new market. This created additional jobs for the poultry producers, the packaging companies, the truck and steamship services that transported the chicken, and the workers who loaded the boxes aboard ship.

The process of growing, manufacturing, storing, and shipping goods makes a neat package. The port's value rises when it can deliver such a package in a speedy, cost-efficient manner.

Future port projects include plans to replace bridges, build industrial parks, install new cranes, improve drainage, and construct new wharves and cruise facilities. And as the mode of freight hauling continues to modernize, port operations will have to accommodate these changes. Eventually trucks and railcars already laden with cargo will be loaded onto ships in Mexico and sent directly to New Orleans. At the dock, they will be unloaded and driven or hauled away immediately, ensuring a speedy delivery to their final destinations.

CHAPTER FOUR

THE BIG EASY

The deck of the **Natchez** *(facing page) gives tourists a river view of the historic city of New Orleans.*

Along with being called the Crescent City for its shape, New Orleans is nicknamed The Big Easy, because life there often happens in a laid-back fashion. On the other hand, like many old-time port cities, New Orleans also has an untamed side. Yet the history of this great port can be summed up in two statements: the Mississippi River gave birth to New Orleans, and commerce helped it grow.

From the start, water and trade have been inseparable from New Orleans. The greater metropolitan area covers 363.5 square miles, only 198.4 square miles of which are dry land. All this water has long been used as a commercial highway, bringing wealth and diversity to the city.

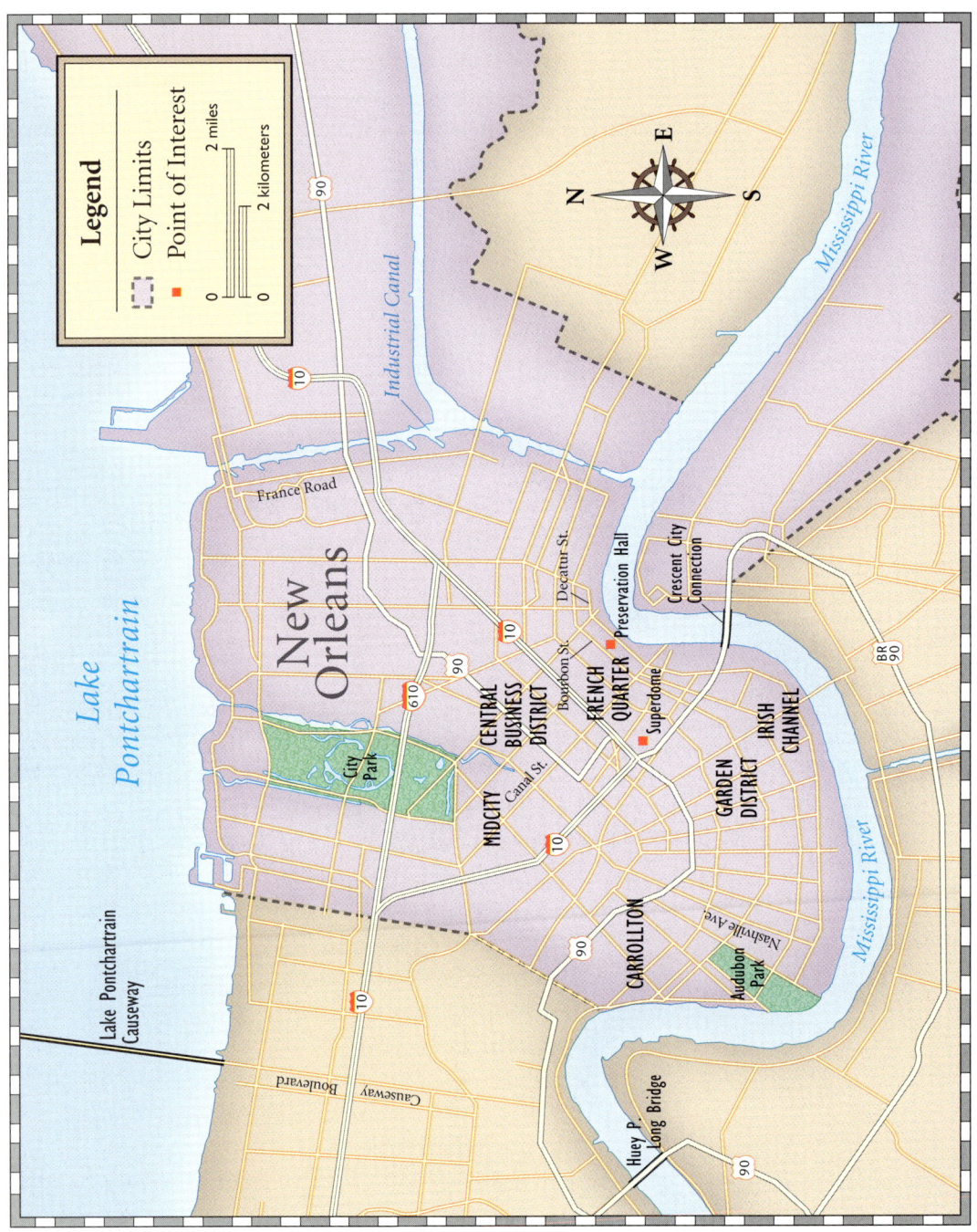

Celebrating Diversity ▶ For centuries New Orleans served as an important gateway to the United States for immigrants from around the world. As a result, the city is one of the most ethnically diverse in the country. Every ethnic group living in New Orleans contributes to the city's distinctive culture.

In the mid-1990s, about 62 percent of the city's total population of 496,938 was African American. Many of their ancestors had been brought to New Orleans as slaves. After the Civil War, when slavery was outlawed, free blacks stayed in New Orleans, contributing to the vibrant cultural mix of the city.

New Orleans celebrates the vast diversity of its population. Here, during the Jazz and Heritage Festival, an African-American vendor sells African-style wares.

At one time, the French Quarter was called Little Italy because so many Italians lived there. The famous Italian Central Grocery on Decatur Street in the French Quarter still sells olive oil, pepperoni, and mouth-watering sandwiches called muffalettos.

Thousands of Germans were among Louisiana's first settlers. So many ethnic Germans lived along the upriver bayous that the area became known as La Côte des Allemands (the German Coast).

The Irish came to New Orleans by the tens of thousands, especially after Ireland's Potato Famine of the 1840s. At that time, disease wiped out Ireland's potato crop and caused widespread starvation. The Irish Channel, a famous New Orleans neighborhood near the Mississippi River, once catered to the large Irish working-class population. Few Irish still live in the Channel.

New Orleans's Latino community makes up only about 3 percent of the city's population. Most Latinos are Hondurans who came to United States in the 1920s to work in and manage warehouses for banana companies. Cubans, Mexicans, Nicaraguans, and others followed. A much larger Latino population lives in the suburbs and neighboring parishes of New Orleans.

A diverse Asian population forms just under 2 percent of the total New Orleans community. Major Asian groups include Vietnamese and Filipinos. Sizable Indian, Japanese, Chinese, Korean, and Pakistani communities are also found in the city.

New Orleans has opened its arms to all these groups and their traditions. Followers of various religions worship in temples, pagodas, cathedrals, and mosques. Restaurants serve Korean kimchi (fermented marinated cabbage), Pakistani *kan-kai-nor-mia* (beef in red curry sauce), Japanese sushi (raw fish), Mexican tortillas, and Irish stews. Several foreign-language newspapers meet the needs of special reader-

▶ Cajuns are descendants of French settlers from Arcadia, a historic region of the Canadian provinces of Nova Scotia and New Brunswick. The largest groups of these settlers came to Louisiana between 1769 and 1785, when the British took over Arcadia and forced the French colonists to leave. Most Cajuns live west of New Orleans.

The French Quarter is famous for its glamorous balconies.

70

ships, and it is not uncommon to find people on the street who speak Spanish, Japanese, Greek, Serbian, Korean, or Chinese.

All this variety is hardly new. New Orleans began as a city made up of many smaller communities. In the old days, wherever there was dry land, settlers built their houses and shops. In contemporary times, the channels, streams, ditches, and marshes that originally divided the city have mostly been filled. But those early natural dividing lines had an impact. Distinct neighborhoods still exist and often trace their origins to a cluster of buildings on one small rise of ground. The Garden District, the Irish Channel, Carrollton, Midcity, and other neighborhoods have their own identities and are proud of their traditions.

A Charmed Life ▶ The city's mix of cultures makes for a sort of New Orleans gumbo—a flavorful local stew. But port cities have reputations as rough, tough, knuckle-knocking hubs. And, as with many modern urban areas, New Orleans struggles with the realities of crime, drugs, poverty, and racism.

Yet few deny that New Orleans is also a delightful charmer. The city's legendary music scene resulted from its mix of heritages. During the slavery period, Africans gathered to dance and sing in Congo Square, just outside the French Quarter. Their African rhythms merged with the sounds of Italian brass bands and other types of music to form the roots of jazz.

As much as New Orleans is celebrated for its colorful history, the city also boasts a vital contemporary life. At night the glitter of skyscraper

lights dapples the water. By day everything is business. Towering office buildings soar where giant cypress and oak trees once stood. Lawyers and businesspeople in dark suits bustle through the Central Business District, called the CBD by locals. Nearby the 27-story Superdome is the city's sports and entertainment center and the home of the New Orleans Saints football team.

While some things have changed in New Orleans, others are reminiscent of the Mississippi's tumultuous old days. Clubs on Bourbon Street in the French Quarter feature performers and great jazz bands. Coffee houses and restaurants are always crowded. Hotels are packed with visitors year-round.

Some of these visitors come as part of the city's highly developed convention trade. But other tourists arrive specifically to partake in New Orleans's numerous celebrations. Be it Mardi Gras or a small neighborhood feast, New Orleans is a city of festivals. Nobody needs an excuse for a party. The New Orleans Jazz & Heritage Festival, the French Quarter Festival, and

A jazz band performs at Preservation Hall (above), *keeping alive the musical tradition of New Orleans. The city's Central Business District* (below) *dominates the New Orleans skyline.*

MARDI GRAS, NEW ORLEANS STYLE

In New Orleans, the most popular event of the year is Mardi Gras. Thousands of folks turn out annually to watch the parades that fill the streets almost daily for two weeks before Fat Tuesday, which is the English translation of Mardi Gras. Traditionally on Fat Tuesday, a fatted calf was butchered for a feast. This feasting occurred because fasting was to follow. In the Christian religion, the season of Lent starts on Ash Wednesday and runs until Easter. Lent involves giving up things and performing good works. In other words, Mardi Gras is a big party leading up to 40 long days of behaving.

During Mardi Gras processions, millions of plastic beads and other trinkets are tossed to the cheering crowd. The yell, "Throw me something, Mister!" is guaranteed to bring results. Krewes, or clubs, sponsor the parades and build marvelous floats. Each krewe has its own costumes and traditions. Elaborately sequined costumes from previous Mardi Gras celebrations can be seen in the old U.S. Mint or the Musee Conti Wax Museum. Rex, who always wears flowing white robes and a crown, is the king of the carnival.

Children in New Orleans eat King Cakes during Mardi Gras. These traditional pastries are frosted with purple, green, and gold icing. A plastic doll is baked inside each cake. Whoever finds the doll is declared "king" of the party and must supply the next cake or throw the next King Cake party.

many other events highlight the city's best music and spicy cuisine. Talented artists enliven stages overlooking the Mississippi, where guitars and clarinets compete with the throaty roars of steamboat whistles.

New Orleans is a popular port of call for cruise lines because of its exciting entertainment, history, and pizzazz. Their fluttering pennants snap in the warm Louisiana breeze from masts that tower above the RiverWalk's mall. The Delta Queen Steamboat Company is also headquartered in New Orleans. From there the 285-foot-long *Delta Queen* steamboat and its two sister ships, the *Mississippi Queen* and the *American Queen,* offer overnight passenger service on the Mississippi River and its tributaries.

Tourism is the second largest industry in New Orleans, following the port commerce. The construction and oil businesses are also crucial to the city's economy. In the mid-1980s, however, the then-booming local economy—anchored in gas and oil—fell into serious decline. Unlike other cities that experienced a

A steamboat ride is a great way to look around the port. The John James Audubon, *the* Cajun Queen, *the* Creole Queen, *and the* Natchez *paddle up and down the river. On afternoon cruises aboard the* Natchez, *a musician plays a powerful steam calliope, or compressed-air organ, on the top deck. Long ago this raucous music heralded the arrival of a riverboat.*

similar **recession,** or downturn in the economy, the citizens of New Orleans did not necessarily leave the city in pursuit of work elsewhere. Consequently New Orleans experienced a high rate of unemployment. Still many residents stayed because New Orleans was their home. While the city has been on the economic mend in recent years, its problems are still numerous.

In 1996 the Port of New Orleans staff moved to a modern building upriver from the French Quarter. The surrounding grounds are like a park, but port managers can simply look out a window toward the Robin Street Wharf and see what's happening on the Mississippi River.

It's been important for the port officials to be close to business on the river. The waterway is always bustling with tugs, towboats, oil-supply vessels, international freighters, military craft, barges, steamboats, and a lone fishing boat or two.

During the summer of 1995, workers "topped out" the new port building, an action that marked the completion of the interior skeleton. On the highest beam of the structure, ironworkers placed an evergreen tree. This tradition dates from ancient Viking times when buildings in Scandinavia were made of wood cut from nearby forests. By placing a tree on a new building, the workers believed that the souls of the dead, who live in the trees, would not disturb the construction. The spirits can find a new home in the evergreen.

Tradition and modern ways. This mixture ensures that the Port of New Orleans will remain viable into the next century.

GLOSSARY

basin: The land drained by a river and its branches.

bayou: A marshy or very slow-moving body of water.

containerization: A shipping method in which a large amount of goods is packaged in large, standardized containers that are easy to transport.

dedicated wharf: A docking point for ships used for loading and unloading a specific type of good.

delta: A fan-shaped deposit of silt and other river sediment at the mouth of a river. The delta divides the river into many smaller channels.

Gulf Intracoastal Waterway: An artificial inland water route along the Gulf of Mexico. The waterway extends from Texas to Florida and passes through New Orleans.

Industrial Canal: An artificial New Orleans waterway that connects the Mississippi River to Lake Ponchartrain.

intermodal transportation: A system of transportation in which goods are moved from one type of vehicle to another, such as from a ship to a train or from a train to a truck, in the course of a single trip.

levee: The natural bank of a river formed during flooding. Artificial levees are constructed to strengthen natural levees in keeping a river's water in its proper channel.

lock: An enclosed, water-filled chamber in a canal or river used to raise or lower boats beyond the site of a waterfall or a set of rapids. Vessels can enter and exit the lock through gates at either end.

Mississippi River–Gulf Outlet (MRGO): The artificial water connection between the Mississippi River and the Gulf Intracoastal Waterway.

North American Free Trade Agreement (NAFTA): A pact between Canada, the United States, and Mexico that went into effect in 1994. The pact created one of the world's largest free-trade zones.

parish: A district in Louisiana that is similar to a county.

protectionism: A trade philosophy of protecting a nation's economy by controlling trade with other countries. Countries that protect their markets often allow only certain types of goods into their country.

recession: A period of time when a community's business sector slows down; is not active.

trade concession: An agreement between countries that outlines the specific trade privileges each nation will award to the other.

PRONUNCIATION GUIDE

Baton Rouge	BAT-uhn ROOZH
Creole	KREE-ohl
Joliet, Louis	JOH-lee-eht, LOO-ihs
La Salle, René-Robert Cavelier de, Sieur	lah SAHL, ruh-NAY-roh-BEHR ka-vuhl-YAY duh, syuhr
Le Moyne, Pierre, Sieur d'Iberville	luh MWAHN, pee-YEHR, syuhr DEE-buhr-vihl
Mardi Gras	MAHR-dee GRAH
Marquette, Jacques	mahr-KEHT, ZHAHK
New Orleans	NOO AWR-luhnz
O'Reilly, Alejandro	oh-RY-lee, ah-lay-HAHN-droh
Pontchartrain	PAHN-chuhr-trayn
St. Domingue	SAN duh-MANG
Tchoupitoulas	chaw-pih-TOO-lahs
Tchoutchouma	chaw-CHOO-mah
Vieux Carré	VYOO cah-RAY

INDEX

Algiers Point, 11, 22
American Revolution, 36
Arabi Terminal and Industrial Park, 27
Arkansas River, 10
Atlantic Ocean, 7, 8
Avondale Shipyards, 52

Barataria Swamp, 28–29
barges, 17–19, 20–21, 56
Baton Rouge, 18, 23, 24
Battle of New Orleans, 44
bayou, 8–9
Board of Commissioners, Port of New Orleans, 64. *See also* Dock Board
Bonaparte, Napoléon, 37, 38
Bourbon Street, 72
Britain, 35, 37–38, 41

Canada, 26, 59, 70
Canal Street, 11, 40
celebrations, 69, 72–74
Civil War, 42–44
coffee beans, 13, 58
Confederacy, 42, 44
containerization, 48
Creoles, 40, 41, 43
Cruise Ship Terminal, 16
CSX Transportation, 19–20
Cumberland River, 10

dedicated wharves, 13
delta, 9, 10
Delta Queen Steamboat Company, 74
de Soto, Hernando, 31
Dock Board, 45–46, 49. *See also* Board of Commissioners, Port of New Orleans
Domino Sugar, 54

economy, 42, 51–52, 55–59, 67, 71–75
Embargo Act, 41

flooding, 11–13, 46
Florida, 10, 16
France, 31–32, 37–39, 41
France Road Wharf, 13, 50–51
French Quarter, 10–11, 34, 40, 69, 70–71, 72

global markets, 58-65
Globalplex Intermodal Terminal, 24, 26
grain, 16, 19, 56
Gulf Intracoastal Waterway, 10, 13, 16, 17, 49
Gulf of Mexico, 7–10, 25, 30, 31, 48, 49

history, 29–49; early settlements, 32–35; European explorers, 30–32; Louisiana Purchase, 37–39; modern times, 48–49; Native American life, 29–30; nineteenth-century growth, 39–42; Spanish rule, 35–37; war and rebirth, 42–47
hurricanes, 12–13

Illinois River, 10
imports, 56–59
Industrial Canal, 12, 13, 16, 17, 48, 49, 50–51
industry, 24–26, 51–55, 74–75
InterCambio 2000, 60–61
intermodal transportation, 48

international trade, 55–62, 64–65

jobs, 51–52
Joliet, Louis, 31

Lake Itasca, 8, 10
Lake Pontchartrain, 8, 11, 12, 17, 34, 35, 46, 47
La Salle, René-Robert Cavelier de, Sieur, 32
LASH vessels, 18–19
Latin America, 54, 56, 58–61
Law, John, 32–34
Le Moyne, Jean-Baptiste, Sieur de Bienville, 32, 33–34
Le Moyne, Pierre, Sieur d'Iberville, 32
levees, 12, 46
locks, 17, 21
Louisiana, 7–8, 21, 32–33
Louisiana Purchase, 37–39

maps, 2, 9, 14–15, 68
Mardi Gras, 5, 32, 72, 73
Marquette, Jacques, 31
MetroVision, 60–61
Mexico, 26, 59
Minnesota, 8–10
Mississippi River, 6–13, 17–18, 22–24, 35, 39, 44–45, 56, 67
Mississippi River Delta, 9, 29–30
Mississippi River–Gulf Outlet (MRGO), 13, 16
Missouri River, 10

Nashville Avenue Wharf, 13, 22
Native Americans, 7–8, 29–30, 34

78

New Basin Canal, 47
New Orleans: ethnic diversity, 69–71; history, 29–49; lay of the land, 6–27; population, 69–70; size, 67; tourism, 72–74
North American Free Trade Agreement (NAFTA), 58–59

Ohio River, 10, 35
oil, 16, 19, 24-25, 55–56, 60–61
Oil Pollution Act of 1990, 53
O'Reilly, Alejandro (Bloody O'Reilly), 35

port facilities, 13–15, 46, 48–49, 52
port management, 20–21, 45–46
Port of St. Bernard, 27
Port of South Louisiana, 24–26

protectionism, 59

Railroads. *See* Trains
recession, 74–75
Red River, 10
religion, 70
River and Harbor Act of 1956, 17
riverboats, 6, 40, 66–67, 74

St. Domingue, 36, 37
Seven Years' War (French and Indian War), 35
shipbuilding, 52–53
Silocaf of New Orleans, 53–54
slaves, 36, 69, 71
Spain, 31, 35–37
steel, 13, 19, 56–57

Tchoupitoulas Corridor, 20–21
Tennessee River, 10
Texas, 8, 10, 16
textile industry, 13, 27
tourism, 72–74

trade, 8, 30, 36–37, 41, 43, 55–62; earliest, 8, 30; international, 55–62, 64–65; Latin American link, 58–61; trade concessions, 36
trains, 19–20, 26, 44
transportation links, 19–20, 26, 48, 56, 59, 65
Treaty of San Ildefonso, 37
tributaries, 9–10
truck lines, 20, 26

unemployment, 75
Union Army, 42, 44–45
U.S. Army Corps of Engineers, 12, 17, 21
U.S. Coast Guard, 22
U.S. Customs Service, 23–24
U.S. Navy, 52–53

War of 1812, 41–42
wharves, 13, 18
World War II, 46, 55

METRIC CONVERSION CHART

WHEN YOU KNOW	MULTIPLY BY	TO FIND
inches	2.54	centimeters
feet	0.3048	meters
miles	1.609	kilometers
square feet	0.0929	square meters
square miles	2.59	square kilometers
acres	0.4047	hectares
pounds	0.454	kilograms
tons	0.9072	metric tons
bushels	0.0352	cubic meters
gallons	3.7854	liters

ABOUT THE AUTHOR

Award-winning author Martin Hintz has written numerous books for young readers and hundreds of magazine and newspaper articles. He is the author of Lerner's *Destination Duluth, Destination St. Louis,* and *Farewell, John Barleycorn: Prohibition in the United States*. Hintz lives in Milwaukee, Wisconsin.

ACKNOWLEDGMENTS

The author would like to thank Peg E. Culligan and Jim Reese of the Port of New Orleans; Tom Hohan of MetroVision; Beverly Gianna and her staff at the New Orleans Metropolitan Visitors and Convention Bureau; and intern Stephanie Schmid. A nod must also go to the dockworkers, tug crews, pilots, men and women of the Coast Guard, shipbuilders, hot sauce manufacturers, coffee baggers, and all the others who offered their insights on the port and its operations. Thanks also to the managers of the Ports of South Louisiana and St. Bernard for their assistance. And another thanks to Continental Airlines, the LaSalle Hotel, and a dozen jambalaya shops in NOLA.